TWO PLAYS

and a

RHAPSODY

KATHARINE HOWARD
Author of "The Book of the Serpent." "Eve," Etc

First Edition

PUBLISHED BY THE AUTHOR AT
SAN DIEGO, CALIFORNIA
1916

THE HOUSE OF FUTURE

In Thirteen Scenes

Written in the ancient forest above the
Castle of Chillon, 1911.

PLACE

The Imagination

No Time — No Plot

CHARACTERS

THE LADY GODELAIRE
THE LORD
YNIDE AND YNIAL—Their Children.
THE OLD NURSE
THE MASTER OF THE HOUSE
—Some may call his name Death and some
may call his name Life—

SCENE FIRST

An ancient forest. A man and a woman, both young, are walking slowly. They are followed by the old nurse of the young woman.

THE WOMAN

This wood is full of mystery. Do you remember the fairy tale about the Princess who slept a hundred years, and how the Prince awoke her with a kiss? I think all women are like that, they sleep until the kiss awakes them. Do you remember how she followed him through all the World, as I would follow you?

THE MAN

One must follow something—as one star wanes another brightens.

THE WOMAN

Once you followed me. What do you follow, now that I follow you?

THE HOUSE OF FUTURE

The Man

Always the thing most beautiful. There is something which calls me on.

The Woman

I also. There is a voice I hear that calls me to high places.

He

You do not understand.

She

Can you not teach me?

He

No—Woman is like a bird, it is but instinct that she has. (*A forest bird sings joyously a little way within the wood.*)

She

And Woman is like a bird? That is a lovely thing for you to say, for birds have wings.

THE HOUSE OF FUTURE

(*She stops to gather moss and shows it to him.*) See, it is like a fairy forest. We are like that fairy tale.—We seek, we know not what, but there is something in this Wood for us to find.

HE

To find and conquer. Man is a conqueror. . . .

SHE

And Woman?

THE MAN

(*Touching her caressingly.*)
She is a slave—

SHE

How do you mean a slave? To Man or Fate?

HE

She is a slave because she is a woman.

THE HOUSE OF FUTURE

She

She is a slave through love—but in the end, if she is like a bird, her wings will free her . . . See! A light falls on the path—we must be near the edges—near that unknown country which lies beyond the wood . .

He

It is a clearing in the forest. Stop a moment and send the Nurse before . . . (*She sends the Nurse before.*) Your hair glows in this light . . . (*He loosens it so that it falls around her.*) You are the fairest woman in the world and you are mine. Guard well your beauty, and if we meet with strangers in the wood, arrange your veil so that they may not see.

She

Sometimes I tremble for fear that you may see a fairer woman.

THE HOUSE OF FUTURE

HE

Have you seen hair longer or silkier or of lovelier colour? Have you seen eyelids longer lashed? Or lips that set a wreath of whiter pearls?

SHE

Sometimes I wish you loved me for my soul, not for my beauty only.

THE MAN

Give me your lips. I love them best when they are silent, pressed to mine. A Woman's mouth is made for love,—except for words of love, speech does not matter. (*They embrace and walking slowly they come into an opening in the wood.*)

SHE

See! the brightness and the towers which rise beyond.

HE

It is a Palace . . .

THE HOUSE OF FUTURE

SHE

A Rose Garden . . .

HE

All is silent,—I see no person.

SHE

But the fountain plays . . .
(*He calls and no one answers . . . He knocks and no one comes.*)

SHE

Here is an inscription. . . . See—it is the House of Future. It is that which we sought unknowing.—But the Master,—where is he?

THE NURSE

My Lady, speak not of the Master, lest one may hear, I know strange legends of this place.

THE MAN

Speak then if there is somewhat that you know.

THE HOUSE OF FUTURE

THE NURSE

I have heard legends.

THE MAN

You have heard, and you have heard. What is it you have heard? What is the Master's name?

THE NURSE

I cannot speak the name lest some one waiteth near—I am afraid.
He tries the door, it opens freely. There is no person there.—Again he calls.— There is no sound but echo.

HE

We will enter, the Master is away.

SHE

Do you not think it is prepared for us?

SCENE SECOND.

The Lady with her old Nurse in the Rose Garden.

THE LADY

I wish my Lord would come. Have you not noticed how my beauty wanes at times?

THE NURSE

No—No—My Lady is most beautiful, the mirror is not true.

THE LADY

My Lord's eyes are my mirror,—I see the waning there. Is it so with all men, that they love beauty only?

THE NURSE

There is a legend that tells how in some distant land across the seas, there is a race of men who are not hunters, and who love faithfully like women.

THE LADY

I wish I knew that land.

THE NURSE

It is a legend.

THE LADY

What name have these strange creatures which my Lord hunts day and night?

THE NURSE

No rightful name that I can speak, My Lady. Some call them birds of pleasure, some birds of prey.—They are not really birds.

THE LADY

I wish my Lord would bring one home for me to see.

THE HOUSE OF FUTURE

THE NURSE

Oh, no! My Lady, they never bring them home. When they have captured them they keep them hidden. They are the creatures of the dark, and lose their beauty in the clear sunlight.

THE LADY

Tell me more of them.—You said there is a legend.

THE NURSE

The legend tells that they are creatures whose souls have been destroyed

THE LADY

How can that be? Souls are eternal.

THE NURSE

I know not,—'tis what the legend tells. The young are beautiful to see and soft to touch. Their beauty does not last because they have no souls.

THE HOUSE OF FUTURE

THE LADY

It is only the beauty of the soul that lasts.

THE NURSE

The legend says.—They bathe themselves in streams and lie among the branches of the trees, letting the long gold tress that grows upon their heads hang down to dry. The legend says. it is this yellow tress which makes the Lords go hunting them.

THE LADY

Why do they live in trees? You said, they are not really birds.

THE NURSE

Because they once had wings, before their souls were killed. I know not,—'tis what the legend tells.

THE LADY

Tell me, tell me, are they Women?

THE HOUSE OF FUTURE

THE NURSE

They might have been had they not lost their souls.

THE LADY

And what becomes of them?

THE NURSE

The legend says, that when they lose their beauty they steal away into the woods and die, or, if they do not die, they become beasts of prey and destroy souls.

THE LADY

I wish that I might help them to get back their souls.

THE NURSE

I have heard,—it was my grandmother who told me,—that once there was a lady who disguised herself, and lived among them hoping to find their souls. It is a long tale, but in the end, the beasts of prey devoured her.

THE HOUSE OF FUTURE

THE LADY

I think it may have been that their souls were taken from them to save them suffering. . . . . How peaceful it is among the roses in this garden. . . . . Come. We will walk in the long corridor. Each day a door swings open at my touch that was firm locked before. Each chamber has been beautiful. Some days I fear to enter—they can not all be so. That door of sandalwood must guard a treasure, the carving is so fine; the hinges and the lock are gold. Perhaps the magic wand is there. I hasten through the other rooms longing for this.

THE NURSE

Unless you find the golden key that fits the lock you cannot enter. . . . Unless— a little child may take you by the hand— Sometimes the key is given to a child . . . The magic wand is in that chamber.

SCENE THIRD

*Several days later in the long corridor.
The Lady Godelaire and the Nurse.*

THE LADY GODELAIRE

Through all the house there is a feeling
that something arrives. Do you not think
the Master comes?

THE NURSE

Ah! The Master,—I have heard,—one
never knows when he is coming except by
signs and omens. I too have had the feeling that something comes—the cat has
washed herself three times this day and
the hounds bayed in the night.

THE LADY GODELAIRE

The hounds bayed? That was because
My Lord returned. (*She touches the doors
on either side of the corridor lightly as she
passes.*) I do not know what has come over

me this day. I have the sense of someone near—and I have heard a fluttering as of wings. . . . *She touches another door,— a narrow white door that shines*—Oh! . . It is this door which opens—a little room —a divan and a mirror,—let us rest and see what happens. . . . It is like a room where one receives. . . . Listen! I hear a sound—it is a little sound. . . . There— again—Do you not hear.

THE NURSE

No—My Lady.

THE LADY (*Listening*)

It is the crying of an infant. It is shut away somewhere.—Oh! . . . It hurts my heart—I must go search for it. . . . Help me to search. (*She listens by the wall.*) It is somewhere through this wall. (*She searches along the wall.*) Ah! . . . this panel is a door—it leads somewhere. But the cry is farther off. . . . Help me to find the cry.

THE HOUSE OF FUTURE

The Nurse

Ah!—My Lady, it is by passing through the torture chamber that you may find it. The cry is in the place beyond. . . . No! My Lady! Do not touch the panel! . . It will open if you touch It is the torture chamber, and they will take away your youth and bits of your beauty —they will tear away with instruments of pain.

The Lady

Oh! . . How do you know this?

The Nurse

There are some things one knows when one is old.

The Lady Godelaire

What shall I do! (*She listens—she hears the cry again.*) Oh! there is something more than beauty. There is something stronger than myself. . . . it is that little cry, it has the force to penetrate these heavy walls. It cries to me, all else is silence beside that little cry which is so mighty that it forces the entrance to my soul. (*She touches the panel.*)

THE NURSE

My Lady! My Lady! the torture! that you must bear alone. . . . .

THE LADY GODELAIRE

It matters not. If I return no more,—adieu. (*She presses the panel, it opens slightly.*)

THE NURSE

Ah! My Lady! do you forget your beauty and my Lord?

THE LADY GODELAIRE

The cry. . . . It is so little that it overwhelms all things. (*She pushes open the panel and goes through. It closes slowly after her.*)

SCENE FOURTH

In the Rose Garden.

The Lord, and the Lady Godelaire. He is about to depart for the Hunt and holds his hounds in leash. The Lady Godelaire wears a long veil of lace that falls from her head and covers all her form.

The sound of distant hunting horns is heard throughout this scene.

THE LORD

Why do you wear the veil? Lay it aside and let you hair fall in this light,—I would compare its length and colour— surely it is the longest. Remove the veil so I may see. (*The horns sound nearer— the hounds pull at the leash. The Nurse comes, bearing in her arms a little child. The Lady smiles and takes the little one into her arms.*)

THE HOUSE OF FUTURE

THE LADY

See! See! My Lord . . . She is far lovelier than ever I have been—it is the little
Ynide.

THE LORD

You should have given me a son to bear
my name.

THE LADY

But you will stay and learn to love her,
will you not?

THE LORD

A Man has other ways of passing time
than nursing infants. (*The child holds up
her arms to him.*) What? What? Now
if it were a son. . . . Well! Well! when
she is grown she may be good to look upon
and make some grand alliance. (*He
throws the leash of his hounds to his serv-
ant and takes the child suddenly into his
arms. She cries. He gives her quickly to
the Nurse and goes. The hounds bay and
the blare of the horns draw near.*)

SCENE FIFTH

*In the Rose Garden. . . . The Lady
Godelaire, the Nurse and the little Ynide.
The Lady Godelaire is touching delicately
upon the strings of her lute a pavane of
the moyen age. . . . The Nurse, after a
limping fashion is showing the little Ynide
the different attitudes of the pavane. . . .
The Lady Godelaire steps the dance as she
touches it out upon the lute. . . .*

THE LADY GODELAIRE

See—it is a lesson Ynide,—hold up your
little gown and try your steps. . . . *The
nurse dances coaxingly before the child.
The scene is charmingly grotesque. . . .
The Lady Godelaire laughs gleefully as
the child dances before the nurse. . .
She moves herself in rhythm with the air.*

THE HOUSE OF FUTURE

The Nurse

In my youth I was held in esteem as a light dancer my Lady. I remember once stepping the dance with one of high degree.

The Lady Godelaire

Indeed, dear Nurse you are even now a brave dancer. . . . Is not the child enchanting? If my Lord were here, how he would love her childish grace. . . .

The Nurse

Three times the hounds bayed in the night. Something will come.

The Lady Godelaire

(*Pushing aside the lute*) We have been many times mistaken. . . . (*The child flutters from rose to rose. . . . The Lady Godelaire and the Nurse watch her intently, their gestures reflect those of the child.*) . . . See how she flies from flower to flower—Ah! she would embrace the fragile things. . . . *The little Ynide runs sobbing to the Lady Godelaire. There is a stain of blood upon her hand.*

THE LADY

No—do not cry—it was a thorn—all roses have their thorns. . . . There, I will kiss the pain away and you shall sleep for I will sing to you. (*She cradles the child in her arms and sings softly an ancient lullaby—to the air of Merlin au Berceau.*) *Dors donc mon enfant mon enfant dors donc.*

SCENE SIXTH.

The same day—in the long corridor. The Lady Godelaire and the Nurse are walking slowly, up and down.

The Lady

Always I feel the sense of someone near —of something mysterious in this house. . . . of things unknown . . . of things that are not seen except through vision of the soul.

The Nurse

One does not reach my age without knowing that there are things unseen.— Beasts are aware. . . . they see the spirits of the dead and they see fearsome things that walk at night and hear them too. . . . Else why would the hounds bay in the night—if there were nothing near?

THE HOUSE OF FUTURE

THE LADY

The hounds bay—dreaming of the Hunt. . . . Ah! When my Lord returns, I hear them far down the forest—heralding his approach.

THE NURSE

I have heard legends. There is that legend of the owl that screeches in the night . . . fearsome it is.

THE LADY

Listen! I thought I heard a sound. . . . (*She pauses in front of the door of the ante chamber. It is the little white door that shines.*) Listen! I thought . . . I thought I heard a sound. . . .

THE NURSE

Ah! Something arrives. . . . (*The Lady Godelaire listens at the door. . . . She pushes—it opens slowly inward.*)

THE HOUSE OF FUTURE

The Lady Godelaire

Ah! it is as I thought. . . . Again the cry. . . . Do you not hear?

The Nurse

No! No! My Lady! the cry is not to me —it is not tuned to me . . . I cannot hear it. (*Impatiently.*) Do not listen—it is enough—you saved the other.

The Lady

Oh! But it pierces through my heart. (*They enter—she sits upon the divan— she listens, she hears the cry.*) . . . Again that torture chamber where all the floor was golden with my hair. . . .

The Nurse

It is below your shoulders now, My Lady and beautiful.

The Lady

I will send some one to save the child.

THE HOUSE OF FUTURE

THE NURSE

No one can find the cry but you, My Lady, no one can hear but you.

THE LADY

Again the cry. . . . No . . No . . . I will not go . . I will not listen. (*She buries her head in the cushions of the divan, but still she hears the cry. She rises and throws aside her veil, her hair falls like a cloud around her—she looks into the mirror . . .*) I have regained my beauty, that I lost.

THE NURSE

But if you lose again you will not, for your youth has gone, it will not come again.

THE LADY GODELAIRE

Listen! Listen! Can you not hear? I know the voice! It is my son who cries to me to bring him to the world!—*She hurries through the door of the torture chamber.*

SCENE SEVENTH.

At night. The chamber of the Lady Godelaire. She stands by a long window which opens on a balcony. A gossamer veil of white is all about her like a cloud. The moon shines on her. . . . The Nurse is on the balcony. Lights from below are reflected on the ceiling of the chamber.

THE NURSE

Yes! Yes! My Lady! It is as I thought, the Master has arrived

THE LADY

No! No! It is my Lord, I hear his voice.

THE NURSE

There is another—do you not hear? . . a slow calm voice of one who has control. . . . It is the Master of the House. . . .

THE HOUSE OF FUTURE

Oh! hide yourself, my Lady. I have heard that each time the Master comes he takes away a guest to his great castle, and they return no more. . . Oh! there are strange tales told, but no one knows the truth . . Some say the castle is so beautiful they will not leave it and they forget, . . . and some, that there are dungeons from which none escape, . . . dark dungeons underneath the ground—so narrow that they can not turn.

The Lady Godelaire

Be still—be still, and let me hear. (*The reflected light of torches passes along the walls and ceiling, a strange heavy sound is heard, and voices.*)

A Voice

I pray you give me time.

Another Voice

You have had time.

THE HOUSE OF FUTURE

THE FIRST VOICE

I pray you give me time to bid the Lady Godelaire farewell.

THE OTHER VOICE

You have had years to say farewell.

THE FIRST VOICE

I pray you, only a moment.

THE OTHER VOICE

My guests await you, you must come with me.

THE FIRST VOICE

I pray you, I pray you, only a moment! I would see the Lady Godelaire to bid adieu—she will wait and wonder that I do not come.

THE OTHER VOICE

She has waited and you have not come.

THE HOUSE OF FUTURE

FIRST VOICE—*Calling*

Godelaire—Godelaire—Adieu! Adieu!
*The lights and shadows pass along the
ceiling. There comes the strange heavy
sound again—and all is silent. . . .*

*The Lady Godelaire recovers as one
awaking from a dream. . . . She rushes
on the balcony and cries*—Adieu! Adieu!
My Lord.—*She returns through the window, weeping.* Oh! My Lord . . . He
has not seen his little son. . . .

SCENE EIGHTH

Some years have passed. The Lady Godelaire talks with the Nurse in the Rose Garden; the roses are withered and the foliage sere. She stands gazing at the withered garden. . . . As she speaks a light shines from her.

THE LADY GODELAIRE

The little Ynide, she suffered. Oh, she suffered, and when He came. He touched her and she smiled and went to sleep. He took her gently while she slept. Just for a moment I saw His face and He seemed neither man nor woman, but an Angel.

THE NURSE

It is the second time and each time in the night. The third time that the Master comes will be for me. The little one will need me. It may be as you think, that He is kind.

THE HOUSE OF FUTURE

THE LADY GODELAIRE

I feel quite sure that He is kind. The little Ynide suffered and He took her pain away. The moment that He touched her the pain was gone. That moment I felt my wings grow strong. I thought I must go with her, but that I could not leave my son. (*A light shines from her as she speaks.*) We will ascend the stairs of the high tower and walk in the Blue Loggia.

THE NURSE

The stairs are steep, my Lady.

THE LADY

And the Loggia high . . . after the dimness of the long ascent it is as Heaven must be. . . . The blue light glows, and afterward it stays with me.

THE NURSE

It is the light within you that shines out, my Lady.

SCENE NINTH.

The Blue Loggia.

The Lady Godelaire and Ynial. She wears a long black mantle—there is a white band about her brow, a white veil falls about her, and a light shines from her as she moves. All around there is a wonderful blue light that scintillates. As far out as she can see, there is the wonderful blue light.

YNIAL

When will you wear your wings again, Mamma?

THE LADY GODELAIRE

My wings, Ynial?

YNIAL

You did not know I saw you for I came softly, and then—I thought you were an Angel, and I went away—I was afraid.

THE HOUSE OF FUTURE

THE LADY GODELAIRE
You would not fear an Angel?

YNIAL

You were different, Mamma, your veil had fallen off, and your black mantle. All I saw was wings and a bright light that shone from you. You talked with some one. . . . Who was there, Mamma? I saw no person. Were you praying? Why do you wear the ugly mantle? It hides your wings,—they looked so soft and beautiful. May I not touch? Where are my wings, Mamma? (*She embraces him.*) Will I not have wings?

THE LADY GODELAIRE

When you are ready for them, but first you have your quest.

YNIAL

What is a quest, Mamma?

THE HOUSE OF FUTURE

THE LADY GODELAIRE

It is a seeking.

YNIAL

Shall I not be a hunter?

THE LADY GODELAIRE

A hunter after stars. It may be that a light will shine for you, and you will seek and find.

SCENE TENTH.

On the stairs of the high tower. The Lady Godelaire and the Nurse.

THE NURSE

My Lady, you should not climb these stairs to the Blue Loggia. The steps grow steeper day by day. My Lady, you are too frail to climb.

THE LADY GODELAIRE

And you, dear Nurse, too old.

THE NURSE

Yes, my Lady,—too old . . . too old . . . I heard my name called in the night. *The Lady Godelaire touches her lovingly.*

THE FLIGHT.

HER VOICE

These blue and amethystine mists that fall beneath us as we cleave the air,—what are they?

THE ANSWERING VOICE

They are the veils of Evening which descend.

HER VOICE

Those shining piled up clouds—are they the mountains of the Dawn? That one with rainbow coloured wings who passed, was he an Angel?

THE OTHER VOICE

A winged soul.

THE HOUSE OF FUTURE

HER VOICE

I see a shining . . . far up among the mountains of the clouds. The columns reach the sun. . . . I see towers beyond towers up-streaking . . . and high arches . . . high arches lessening down the vista of their aisle. . . . Towers transcendently entrancing. Towers of my dream woven radiant city . . . and those far reaching dim islands of the sky . . . cloud islands of my dreams. My vision is made whole. . . . Every motion of my wings enhances the radiance of those towers. . .

Towers of Enshrinement, are they not? May I fly there?

THE ANSWERING VOICE

There is no limit.

HER VOICE

I have no weariness, I am all ecstacy and luminous. I do not need to speak, only to think. Are all the angels so?

THE HOUSE OF FUTURE

Have they one language of the soul? I was afraid to fly, but when you touched me all my fear was gone,—I could fly fast and free. . . . Ah! . . . My memory comes— You are the Master of the House. . . . How strange I should forget—But with my memory my weariness returns. . . . Where is My Lord?

THE OTHER VOICE

You will forget him, until his soul has gathered strength to waft his wings.

HER VOICE

There is a weight that pulls me down, —it drags my left wing down. . . . I hear a voice that calls to me. It is the voice of Ynial. Where is the little Ynide?

THE OTHER VOICE

Where the great shining is among the pillars reaching to the Sun.

HER VOICE

I hear the voice of Ynial. I will go

back to the Blue Loggia and put away my wings. May I go back?

THE OTHER VOICE

Much is given to the souls of Mothers. I will wait until you call and come again for you.

THE VOICE OF YNIAL

Mother! Oh! I have called and called— and could not waken you. . . . I found you lying here, close to the step that leads into the blue. At first I thought there were two Angels—but there is only you. . . . Mother! You should have been awake to see. The wings were shining everywhere. . . .

SCENE TWELFTH.

Many years have passed.
The Lady Godelaire and Ynial in the
Rose Garden by the fountain.

YNIAL

Mother—I have heard a voice. It called
to me to come and do my work. To me
alone it called . . . Something is lost
which I must find—and Mother I saw a
light that shone—it seemed to make a path
for me. . . . It was the same light that I
have seen shining from you.

THE LADY GODELAIRE

My son. . . . *She presses her head*
against his shoulder.

YNIAL

No—do not fear. I will not go, I will
not leave you here alone. My Mother.

THE HOUSE OF FUTURE

THE LADY GODELAIRE

You must go, Ynial. You have seen the light and you must follow where it leads. . . . I will be there, Ynial. . . . Come to the Blue Loggia after a little, and you will understand. (*She embraces him.*)

SCENE THIRTEENTH

YNIAL—*Alone.*

She is not here. . . . No. She is not
here. . . . Her mantle—and her veil—
close to the step that leads into the blue.
. . . Ah! I understand—it was for me
she staid . . . Now I remember the angel
and the light. She was the Angel—but I
did not know because she hid her wings.
. . . Now I understand. She wore the
mantle to conceal herself. . . .

He gazes far out into the blue.

Again I hear the call. . . . There are
wings all about me. . . . I hear. . . . I
hear—It is more than music—and I see—
I see the light. . . . It is herself—She is
the light—and she has gone to show the
way. . . .

*Chords of celestial music sound from
afar—nearer and nearer they sound—ab-
sorbing and surrounding all.*

THE HOUSE OF LIFE.

KATHARINE HOWARD

THE HOUSE OF LIFE

Written February 1910.
Beuzec—Conq—par Concarneau, Bretagne, France.

SCENE—EARTH

An Old Person. A Young Person and
the one with echoing footsteps

THE HOUSE OF LIFE

TWO PERSONS. ONE OLD AND ONE YOUNG

THE OLD PERSON—*says*

No! No! My child, pray do not enter there.

THE YOUNG PERSON

Oh! but I must, I am compelled, a spirit leads me.

OLD PERSON

What does the spirit say, my child?

YOUNG PERSON

The spirit says—This is the house of Life—enter, it says.

OLD PERSON

Oh! but knock on the door my child— knock thrice upon the door.

THE HOUSE OF LIFE

Young Person

There is no need to knock, the door is swinging open. Come—enter you—I would not be alone—still, I am not afraid. *They enter.*

Old Person

No—do not close the door—the entrance is so dark. . . . How dark the hall, and narrow.

Young Person

Here is another door, the key is in the lock. . . . I am afraid! Let us turn back. Oh! Oh! I cannot see the way—the entrance door is swinging shut. . . .

Old Person

The door has shut, we must go on.

Young Person

Open you, this door. The key is rusty in the lock. . . How the door creaks.

THE HOUSE OF LIFE

OLD PERSON

Here is a stairway—let us mount. . . .
See how worn the steps. How many feet
have climbed them. . . .

YOUNG PERSON

There is no one now—we are alone.

OLD PERSON

I have a strange weird feeling—as if I
had been here before, a feeling that I cannot speak—like a foreboding that something tragic lies beyond. . . I wish we
had not entered here. . . . I wonder—is
it a dream or is it real. . . . Here is a tablet in the wall—read you—I am too old, I
cannot see. . . . What says the tablet?

YOUNG PERSON

The few go on—the many pause. There
are but two ways now—either go up—or
through this door. . . .

OLD PERSON

I see no door.

THE HOUSE OF LIFE

Young Person

It is a secret door and hard to see.

Old Person

Where does the door lead—does it say?

Young Person

No—not in words—there is an arrow pointing down. . . . I am afraid—let us go on.

Old Person

Yes—we will climb these stairs—these stairs are little worn. . . . Do you hear footsteps?

Young Person

They are echoes.

Old Person

Listen! I thought I heard a voice. . . .

Young Person

Only the echo of our own. . . . Come

THE HOUSE OF LIFE

—are you tired—the reason why you
mount so slow—so wearily?

Now we have reached the landing. See
what a broad and sunny hall!

Old Person

It seems quite pleasant, but we do not
know what lies beyond.

Young Person

No need to think of anything beyond—
we will stay here where it is pleasant. . . .
Oh! There is a door that looks as if it led
into a closet. I will open it and see.

Old Person

No! No! My child! You frighten me!
Open no closets I pray—I pray you keep
the closets closed—I would the doors were
sealed.

Young Person

They may be full of treasures.

THE HOUSE OF LIFE

OLD PERSON

It is better not to know. . . . It is no echo. I hear a footstep. . . . There—do you not hear it? Now—it is coming nearer.

YOUNG PERSON

I feel that I have always heard it. . . . It comes for me. . . .

OLD PERSON

How long it seems since we two entered here. . . .

YOUNG PERSON

Yes, it was long ago. You must stay here and rest for you are tired. I will go to meet him. When you are rested we will return for you. . . .

OLD PERSON

It is the echoing footstep of my foreboding. Always the echo. . . . Do not go. *She goes to meet him. They pass on to-*

*gether through the house of Life. They come to a sunny window with a broad seat—cushioned soft and deep. . . . He says,—*Let us rest here.

SHE

Yes—we will rest here. From this window we can see across the valley to the far hills.

HE

Now there are clouds—dark clouds—and now the rain. . . . We can see nothing now—save through the mist

SHE

But we are happy—sunshine or rain—we are together.

HE

The cushions here are soft. We will stay here. The clouds are passing. . . . How fertile the valley is.

SHE

This is a strange lovely room—it is full

of beauty. I will see what is contains. *She wanders restlessly about the room.* Here is a picture in a frame of gold.

HE

What says the picture?

SHE

It is the window scene, but far more beautiful.

HE

How can that be. How can it be more beautiful?

SHE

I know not—but it is. . . . It speaks to me of dreams and lovely thoughts. It rests me into happiness. . . . *He comes and looks with her.*

HE

Yes—it is beautiful. It is the artist's soul that speaks to us. We think his thoughts and share his ecstacy. What is the name across the corner—can you make it out?

THE HOUSE OF LIFE

A silken curtain slowly draws before the picture.

SHE

I do not like these drawing curtains and these closing doors.

HE

There are few pictures on these walls— they have been taken down and stand in corners—turned toward the wall.

SHE

Let us go on—these drawing curtains please me not.

HE

The window seat is pleasant. Why look! The curtains are drawn there. Why did you close them?

SHE

I did not close them. Come let us go. We have been a long time here.

HE

Let us go on. How many corridors

there are—and all must lead somewhere.
. . . So many doors and each one different.

SHE

We will go through this corridor, the
carpet here is softer for our feet—it must
lead to some stately chamber. . . .

Here is the door—how fine the carving
is—I am half afraid of doors—you open it.
*He opens the door into the Hall of Mir-
rors.*

SHE

Oh! How enchanting—how glad I am
we chose this corridor. . . . Now I can see
myself in every way. . . . There are closets
between the mirrors—there must be lovely gowns. I will array myself.

HE

No! No! You please me as you are.

SHE

There is fascination in these mirrors. I

never looked so well before. Do you not think so?

He

I see no difference. Let us go on, there is nothing here but glitter.

She

See! There is another woman—it was not myself I saw—There is another! And another! Fairer than I. They are looking at you from the mirrors. They seem to know you. Who are these women?

He

I see no woman there but you. . . . But there are men.

She

The reflections of yourself. . . . The hall seems full of people. They are reflections of the people who have looked into these mirrors. . . .

He

The reflections of our other selves.

THE HOUSE OF LIFE

SHE

How cloudy the mirrors grow—a mist
has come upon them.

HE

Come away. I do not see you in the
mirrors now. I see a woman old and worn.

SHE

Let us go quickly. I am so tired of
mirrors. I wish there were no mirrors
in the world. See! . . . there are cobwebs
hanging from the frieze. I am afraid.
Why did we come into this hall. I wish
that you had chosen some other corridor.

HE

There is no one here, and yet I feel as
if we pushed our way among a crowd. Is
it so with you?

SHE

Yes, yes—give me your hand and let
us hasten. These are dead pleasures—the

struggling ghosts of long dead pleasures —trying to bar our pathway. . . . I hear a sound of weeping. Ah, me! I hear the voice of a young child. This is a house of grief. I wish the entrance door had been thrice barred against the time I entered here. . . . Those women were so fair. They seemed to know you.

HE

All this is fantasie—a spell has come upon you.

SHE

Alas! There is no other door—we must return through the dead pleasures and the misty mirrors. Let us go quickly. . . . Those women beckon you. Let us go quickly from this place. . . . *They pass back through the carved door into the corridor. The door closes silently behind them. They come to a gothic archway and go through into the place of Meditation. There is absolute silence. After a time a sound comes out of the silence.*

THE HOUSE OF LIFE

She

Listen! Do you not hear? It is far off.

He

No—it is near. It is like the wind in a great forest. . . . Or like the rhythm of the surf.

She

It is like the song of birds in the springtime of the World. . . . It rests me after the bewilderment of mirrors. . . . These gothic arches are all one with the sound.

He

They are the overcurving branches of forest avenues. The roof.

She

It is too much of ecstasy—it cannot last. (*The music grows more solemn and majestic. . . . It is a funeral march.*)

Always this suggestion in the house of Life. . . . There—it is over, it seemed a thousand years.

THE HOUSE OF LIFE

HE

It was because we heard the echoes of the aeons since Time began. The Funeral March of Time passing to Eternity. . . . *The light grows dim. They go out and the doors clang shut behind them.*

SHE

Why can we never stay—why must we be forever moving on—why must we leave the pleasant places?

HE

Where are the others who have gone before?

SHE

Here is a door with writing on it. Do not hurry—let me look—(*She reads*—The Closet of the Secrets—Open Not—*She turns the key—the door opens slowly inward of itself—He tries to draw her away but she will look. . . . She clings to him pale with fright.*) Ah, me! Ah, me! Why

did I ever live to know such horror! . . .
She told me not to look—she must have
known—and you? You knew and yet you
live? Are all the closets full of horror?

HE

I am a man—and strong, all men must
know.

SHE

Where is the woman who entered here
with me? So long ago it was, I left her
there to rest. . . I had forgotten her. Take
me to her.

HE

You had forgotten her? . . . Who was
she?

SHE

Take me to the place where I left her.
The doors! It may be that the doors are
barred. *They find their way back to the
place where she had left the woman. She
is not there.*

THE HOUSE OF LIFE

HE

It is so long ago. Where can she be?

SHE

The secret door at the foot of the stairs. She may have gone that way. . . . Yes here it is—it has been opened—she has gone this way. *She opens the door—it opens hard. . . . A cold mist rises that chills them both with dread. . . . They see only a few steps leading down and all below is dark. . . . An invisible something rushes past them through the open door —the house is filled with muffled footsteps and whispering voices.*

SHE

Close the door. Oh! Close it quickly.

HE

But the voices and the footsteps—we cannot drive them back to the place whence they came—already the house is filled with them.

THE HOUSE OF LIFE

SHE

Oh why did I forget. How long ago it seems—how tired she must have grown of waiting. How kind she was—now I remember when it is too late.

—They cannot close the door, and chilled with the damp mist, they climb the stairs again. The steps grow steeper as they struggle up. No corridors entice them— they keep on until they reach the roof of the house. As they go up the doors clang shut behind them—there is no going back.

HE

What now? The night is dark.

SHE

I see a star. . . . Look! There are many stars.

They wait upon the roof.

A RHAPSODY

Written in Florence, Whitsuntide, 1912.

KATHARINE HOWARD

A RHAPSODY

The Spirit of the Future took the Poet
by the hand and walked with him. . . .
They walked along the edges of the tides
in the shadow of great cliffs until they
came to the Place of Caverns—and they
went into that cavern where the echoes of
the Past were sleeping. . . . The Spirit
said,—tread lightly that we may not wake
these echoes before they are refreshed.
It is not time to wake them, it is the early
dawn. There are great things to do, and
if we wake them they will disturb us with
complainings—they need to sleep until the
light is strong so they may see to find their
places in the Harmony.

And so—because the time was not yet
come to wake the echoes of the Past—the
Poet walked in silence—but he thought

great thoughts—and when the silence overpowered him he expressed himself in sculpture or painted beauty which revealed his soul.

———

Again the Poet walked, and after wandering through the night he came to the place where the Queen of Dawn sat on a hill—around her were the girls of Morning—burnishing and braiding the gold strands of her hair. . . .

Down in the valley—the simple people said,—it is sun-fire that burns,—but to the Poet, knowledge was given by the desire for beauty—and he alone of all men knew it was the shining of her hair. . . . From looking at the bright strands of her hair streaking the mists of Dawn—he grew a keener vision—he saw halos around the heads of Mothers and their children—and wings that drooped from shoulders of young maidens—and youths who wore their swords of destiny sheathed on in chastity. . . . Deep in the eyes of old men, he could read the broader knowledge which they had of Life—the gracious charity and insight which their years had given them in judging the affairs of youth.

It was Whitsuntide, and the Poet walked the streets of a great city. The people were crowded and pressed together everywhere and all the air was full of particles of unclean dust.

Around the city there was a circle of green hills and there were trees and brooks and many flowers—but when the Poet looked he saw no people there,—and while he wondered, a little child came to him and took his hand and walked with him among the crowd. They walked together a long way,—so that the child's hand grew warm in his, and beat with the same pulse.

They came before a vast cathedral and the little child pulled at his hand and led

A RHAPSODY

him in. . . . There, in a great space in the centre, walled about with glass, were many priests in vestments made of cloth of gold and wrought with precious gems, —and one priest sat on high before them with all his garments spread in a great glory and on his head a jeweled crown. Wreaths of incense arose from swinging censers and myriads of candles burned . . .

The priests bowed themselves in curious fashion and moved about continually, and as they moved a flood of music filled the place and rolled among the arches and possessed his soul with beauty. . . . Time was as nothing—and when he looked again . . . it may have been a thousand years . . . the little child was gone—the music ceased—and while he looked upon the bowing vestments—there came a sense of vacancy and he looked closer and saw that they were empty—there was no life no soul in them—they were nothing but empty vestments that moved themselves from habit. . . . And he went out again

into the street searching his lost illusion
and the little child.

————

Again the Poet walked—unconscious
of surroundings,—for he was thinking
deeply.

He walked until there came to him a
feeling of great rest . . . sweet odours
soothed his senses and the air was fresh.

He paused to look upon the world and
found that he had climbed a mountain,
and yet he had the sense of rest. . . . He
remembered that somewhere in a mountain dwelt the spirit of Eternal Youth.

Far down within the valley he saw the
city shining in a golden mist,—her domes
and towers fantastically grouped—and all
the unclean dust that rose from her,
touched into beauty by the magic of the
sun.

The while he thought upon this thing
and wondered,—there came the longing

for that young boy whose hand had been so warm in his.

And while he thought, two girls came running, and pointing to the city, called, —behold the beauty that shineth far below! We are the slaves of a young boy and can not go. . . . Down in the city where the beauty is,—his enemy awaits to slay him.

Is he the spirit of Eternal Youth? the Poet asked.

Yes, but he sleeps,—they answered,— and so we gaze upon the city where we long to go.

Show him to me,—the Poet said.

And when he looked upon the sleeping boy, he recognized him for the same who walked with him, that Whitsuntide, the streets of the great city.

CPSIA information can be obtained
at www.ICGtesting.com
Printed in the USA
BVHW041702161019
561264BV00003B/114/P